pretty puppy

Think of a name for the puppy and write it in the panel below the picture, then colour the picture frame.

1

whose ball?

Find the puppy stickers and draw a line to match each puppy to its ball.

1

2

a

b

3

c

d

4

Answer: 1 - d, 2 - a, 3 - b, 4 - c.

How many puppies?

Find the stickers and count the puppies in each basket.

a

b

c

d

Answers: a - 2, b - 5, c - 1, d - 3.

2

Perfect pairs

Find the stickers and then draw lines
to join the matching puppies.

a

b

c

1

2

d

e

3

4

5

COOl POOdiES

Can you find four differences in the picture on the right?

shopping list

Find the stickers and tick the boxes
for each item on the shopping list.

✳ Shopping list

- bowl ☐
- collar ☐
- food ☐
- lead ☐
- bed ☐

Let's play!

Draw a picture of this puppy playing.

Odd one out

Which spotty puppy is the odd one out?

1 2 3 4 5

5

What's next?

Find the stickers to complete these patterns.

1

2

3

Answer: 1 - hoop, 2 - yellow bone, 3 - orange ball.

Brilliant balloons!

Follow the key below to colour these balloons:

1 - blue
2 - pink
3 - purple
4 - yellow

spot the difference

Can you find four differences in the bottom picture?

Fluffy friends

Find the stickers to see what present this puppy has given to each friend.

chase the ball

For 4 players

Press out the counters on the press-out page and find a dice. Each player chooses a counter and places it on 'Start'. Take it in turns to throw the dice; the first person to roll '6' moves first. Take it in turns to roll the dice and move your counters around the board. If you land on a forfeit do what it says and miss your next go. The first player to catch the ball is the winner.

↳ dice

36 Finish	35	34	33 Shake hands with the person on your left!	32 Say your favourite colour!	31
25	26 Do a ballet twirl!	27	28	29	30 Woof a song – can anyone guess it?
24 Stand on one leg and count to 10!	23	22	21 Neigh like a horse!	20	19
13	14 Cluck like a chicken!	15	16	17 Tell an animal joke!	18
12	11	10 Think of five puppy names!	9	8	7 Don't speak for the rest of the game only sing!
1 Start	2	3 Do an impression of your favourite animal!	4	5	6 Try to touch your nose with your tongue!

8

Press out counters for the game on page 8.

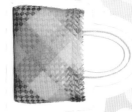

Create your own cuddly puppy tales!
Press out the pieces and fold all tabs back
to make your play pieces stand.

To make this pretty trinket tray, press it out and follow the instructions below.

1. Push tabs through slots first.

2. Dab glue to inside tabs and press to secure. Leave to dry.

add glue here

add glue here

slot

add glue here

add glue here

slot

Press out the door hanger, decorate with stickers and hang on your door!

Match patch

Find the stickers to complete these pictures.
Which puppy is the odd one out?

1

2

3

4

Answer: 1 because he is standing up.

In the park

Puppy is playing ball in the park.
Draw and colour the background.

Play day maze

Help the tired puppy home after a busy day playing.
Find the stickers to see what toys the puppy played with.

Start

Finish

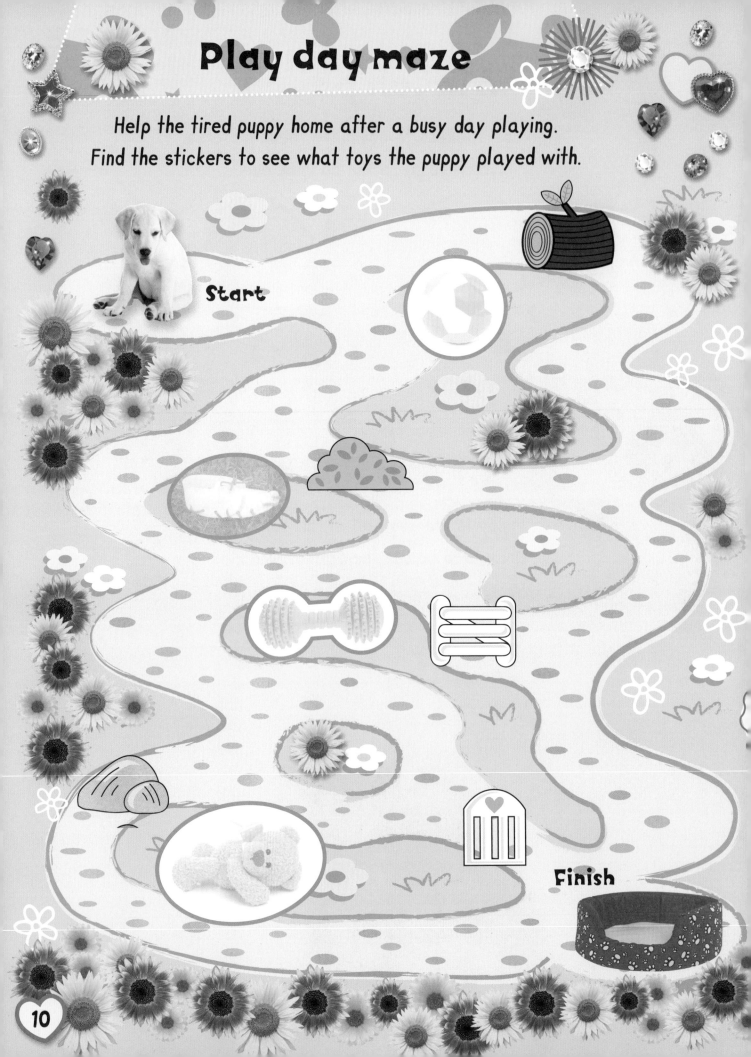

FLOWER PUPPIES

Join the dots and then find
the puppy stickers.

How many bones?

Find the stickers and follow the lines to see
which puppy has the most bones?

a

b

c

d

11

Let's count

How many toys, combs and food bowls can you count?
Write the numbers in the boxes.

PUPPY dreams

Draw a picture to show what this puppy is dreaming about.

Answer: toys - 3, combs - 6, bowls - 5.

12

Puppy pairs

Find the stickers to complete the pictures. Which pair of puppies is the odd one out?

1

2

3

4

Answer: pair 2 because they are lying down.

What's for tea?

Find the stickers and follow the lines to see what each puppy is dreaming of for their dinner.

a

b

c

Answer: a - biscuits, b - cheese, c - bone.

Happy birthday

The puppies are having a birthday sing-a-long. Follow the lines to each puppy's present. Can you guess what they are?

a

b

c

1

2

3

Answer: a – 2 (bowl), b – 3 (ball), c – 1 (bone).

name the puppy

Find the stickers and give each puppy a name.

Finish the pictures

Find the stickers to complete these
pictures, then colour the background.

DRAW and colour

Join the dots and colour the puppies.

Goodbye!